AF612629

SONGS OF A STRANGER AT THE SMILING COAST

SONGS OF A STRANGER AT THE SMILING COAST

Poems

OBINNA CHILEKEZI

Published by
Kraft Books Limited
6A Polytechnic Road, Sango, Ibadan
Box 22084, University of Ibadan Post Office
Ibadan, Oyo State, Nigeria
+234 (0) 803 348 2474, +234 (0) 805 129 1191
+234 (0) 803 350 9421 +234 (0) 905 723 9357
Email: kraftbooks@yahoo.com
kraftbookslimited@gmail.com
website: www.kraftbookslimited.com

© Obinna Chilekezi

First Published 2020

ISBN: 978-978-918-603-7

= KRAFTGRIOTS=
(A literary imprint of Kraft Books Limited)

All Rights Reserved

First Printing, February, 2020.

Dedication

This collection is dedicated to the memory of my father, Nze Julius Ukah Chilekezi

Fair seedtime had my soul, and I grew up
Fostered alike by beauty and by fear;
Much favoured in my birthplace, and no less
In that beloved Vale to which, erelong,
I was transplanted ...
—WILLIAM WORDSWORTH, The Prelude

Contents

Introduction

One of the biggest challenges I always have after putting together a work like this together is to write an introductory remark to it. This may not be unconnected to the fact also that I always find it difficult to even introduce myself. I normal fall short of words to say who I am. Should I start by talking of my background in librarianship, of that of journalism or should I begun on insurance which had until the recent time given a career that I can be proud of. I feel this also applies to my poetry, as a writer I find equally difficult to compartmentalize my poems. I write poems as the thoughts flow in me. Incidentally this is the first time that I have decided to challenge myself to work with a specified period of time an anthology that tries to have a common focus, which incidentally is the Gambia.

My love for the tourist country came accidently, as I had little or no knowledge of that country until I was invited there to take up an appointment as a visiting lecturer at the

West African Insurance Institute some years back. Loneliness and the beautiful weather then prompted me to take up the saddle and write again poems again and again. This has been an abandoned hobby for some time back. Thanks to The Gambia that has made me to know that I cannot come back to the literary family just like a prodigal that had abandoned home only to discover it in a faraway land.

I have to confess The Gambia is a beautiful country with a people that are homely and friendly to a fault. It is a country, you visit and feel at home in it too. Not to talk of its coasts, rivers, birds and butterflies. I have not only visited the country, I have travelled in it from Banjul to Basse, which is just like from the beginning to the end. It is indeed a beautiful country, like it and I Know if you try, you will also do. I can use the famous word of John Keats to describe my feelings of the country as follows:

Much have I travelled in the realms of gold,
And many goodly states and kingdoms seen;
Round many western islands have I been

Which bards in fealty to Apollo hold.

Oft of one wide expanse had I been told

That deep-browed Homer ruled as his demesne;

Yet did I never breathe its pure serene

Till I heard Chapman speak out loud and bold:

Then felt I like some watcher of the skies

When a new plant swims into his ken;

Or like stout Cortez when with eagle eyes

He stared at the Pacific – and all his men

Looked at each other with a wild surmise -

Silence, upon a peak in Darien.

–John Keats

I must also state that the beautiful word of William Cowper in his poem *Charity*, written in the eighteen century also apply to The Gambian coast, as he wrote:

Ingenious Art, with her expressive face,

Steps forth to fashion and refine the race; ….

Hers is the spacious arch, the shapely spire,

The painter's pencil and the poet's lyre;

From her the canvas borrows light and shade,
And verse, more lasting, hues that never fade ….
Where commerce has enriched the busy coast.

I saw all these at various places in the small island country, yes the spacious arches admired in ruins while entry Banjul from the mainland; or the mosques ever big and adorned shapely spires and the beauty as penciled by nature along the coast striving with commerce for tourist patronage.

This form of wonderful feeling I had first time in The Gambia and more so, it was not a Chapman to speak out and loud on such beauty but I as the watcher. I had documented this experience in poems. Some of the poems that I wrote there are also in my collection, My Gambia and other Poems and also published in journals like the Better than Starbucks and the online publication Africa Forum, A Collection of Poems: A diverse Collection of Poems I like, PoemHunter.com , among others. It is here I begin to experience with a new voice, African voice, in my poetry.

It is the Gambian nature I tried to document here, a form of imitation of what I saw at various places. The eye of a poet is just like a lens that captures scenes visible and invisible which are painted on canvass using words. Little wonder then that Wordsworth had posited that "The tendency of metre is to divest language in a certain degree of its reality, and thus to throw a certain half-consciousness or unsubstantial existence over the whole composition". This is the feeling of the stranger at the smiling coast mirroring the feeling of a Nigerian at The Gambian coast falling in love with its river and its damsel. I am a witness and just a witness.

The poems of the poet have appeared in serials like Daily Times, Times International, Rake and ANA Review. Some of them have appeared in these anthologies: Twenty Nigerian Writers (ANA Lagos), For Ken, For Nigeria (E. C. Osondu), New Nigerian Voices (Gloria Monica Emezue) and Passport to the New WWorld) Sunny Ayewanu). I will also like to use to thank my Gambian friends like the WAII DG Mr Fredrick Bowen-John and other staff of the Institute like Mr Omotowa and Mr Lamin. I will not forget these people I disturbed for meaning of Wolof words like Alhaji M Joof, Delight Ezeh, Jankey Jargu, Patience Johnson, Mariatou Jawo. I must confess that each time I ask for the Wolof meaning of words I will get different spelling of the same word, for instance the word river which my editor said I should change to Wolof: Gage, Gaugil, Gaygi and I had to go with that of the English Wolof Dictionary which stated it as Geej. You can understand my plight! I will also like to thank Mariatou Jawo for the permission to use her photograph for the cover.

Finally, to use the words of the Nigerian poet, Okinba Launko: "so, come, travel along with me now as I did, and discover the songs" of this stranger at the smiling coast.

Love

Do I need further reason

Do I need further reason to explain
Why I should stay here in the smiling coast
Leaving behind my town just for hers,
Swim with her along the flow of the river Gambia
Watching in lust,
the waves of her river waving up and down the flow
And the sweet air, from nowhere, begin to blow
It blew cold winds, cooling the suburb
And dissolving my thought of home
The day then battles the cold around,
It was a very cold afternoon to behold

It was not too long ago, I 've owed all apology
For apparently abandoning my home for that of hers
But here I am, far far far away from home,
with an abandoned apology in my pocket
May be I too has been kept a prisoner by Calypso, the witch of love
And the Greek Poseidon had abandoned me to fate

The Greek gods are not to be blamed, neither mine too
The gods have abandoned me to fate, and to my faith
Please blame not the gods,
Blame me mortal for my harvest from my sowings
For I was the one that invited the bright eyes of Calypso to my abode
It has kept me a prisoner at Troy
Blame not the gods

Brothers see me counting one by one the seagulls at her river bank
And the sands at the bank of the smiling coast of The Gambia
This has further distanced the road to home from my sight
But I know, one day I must go home to the river Niger

Maybe after the whirlwind of the storms

Striking my memory to life again
Its effect very disturbing with a killing memory to withstand
Just as the stars in the sky in a conflict to watch,
I have seen this and more in life
But there still tempting, sprouting out again and at sight
Beautiful sea-side flower of the Gambian coast,
Its fragrance better than that of the Niger

I stood,
I remembered the cries of Xenophobia in a distant land from here,
I stood,
I weep, I am confused
Thinking of home
My home with this grip of Calypso too strong to let go
Yes it has been too dangerous, leaving one's own home
For a town like this,
In this moment and in a stolen desire

I wake up, another dream of you.

Each day

I have traversed your land
I have seen your sun rise
And set on your face

Each day

I have seen undiluted smiles
Across your rural counties,
Your micropolitan areas along the rivers

Each day

I saw hunger, naked on the streets,
Been worn like a strange clothe
By urchins, with infectious smiles

Each day

But their quench hunger, disproportionate in size
Could not their envious smiles
As laughers rise with the rising sun

Each day

(07/09/19)

I was too far to understand

the rains are here
and Banjul is still real hot to stay
for I had dreamt of you with flowers in hands
waiting, waiting for me as promised
only to meet today that your summer had left for the moon
with the endless love of you for me
all gone for a wild life vacation

hold on, hold on my lady
just when I needed you in my mind
could this be the promise that had flown me into your nest
in this season
season when the flowers bloom and bloom with lipstick red smiles
and the birds in their beautiful coloured feathers
fly around the sky, songfilled

lady
am I living in our shared past
thinking it the present and future, just a dream
when your laughter had ploughed the smile from the moon
place it on the bed of the river Gambia as it flows
and you and I sharing a wet kiss
while unveiling this strange world, now

today presence is really hot, its hot as
the heat of Banjul's sky, indeed it is
difficult for me to comprehend
tell me, tell me how best a lover could love love
when love had gone on a strange journey, it is absent now and here
for without you Soxna
the moon has no life, it has no light, it is empty

without asking and you know, lady

your name is ringing the bells of birdsongs we shared
your presence remains my favourite midnight movie
as I stand here and stare in wait of you
leaving with dreams of wanting to kiss another, yes very tempting
then our vow, I vowed to kiss the river Gambia again and again
thereby in its bank, I stand, starring at the stars, confused

the stream still sails as ever
but along its coast sandprints of our former presence
signs of our hurriedly kisses before the watery presence
now the footprints on the sand, you left
yes the footprints on my heart, you left
when your briefly left, are still there starring to the stars
I am looking at some of them, as I wait for you

the night is coming too close to dawn
here I am, still shocked by the pains you left for me behind
as you run wildly to your underground river
I should have seen this earlier, with
the dark colours deeming your smile last time we met
a language, a sign and a message
that I was too far carried away to understand.

12/10/19
BANJUL

Indeed in the season

We are in the season of smile
The marigold flowers smiles across the way
And the trees as green as trees are to be

The songbird
Wakes up in the season's morning
And weaved its songs to the sun

The sun smiles
Sparkling with its spherical yellow tooth
At the peak of the morning

Two strange lovers
Secretly exchange kisses at the river bank
Leaving behind strong shadows as witness

Indeed we are in the seasons of smiles
The songbird weaves sunshine songs, for
Two strange lovers to secretly kiss each other with smiles.

02/09/19

As earth moves on

I have desired you, as
The Sahara desert desires your river Gambia
For just those your sparking drops of sweat smiles
But then you changed your gear, reversed it
To direction, yet unknown to me
And the sun kept its movement, on and on to no end
Here am I
Standing at that bank that we had shared moon and star lights together
Thought of you, without you filled the moment
What a killing terror, to behold; it is even not bearable
Let me make this elegy now, before the passing sad winds
As the love we had known, before is gone to the winds
While the earth continue to move on just like the sun.

28/09/19
Banjul

For love can be a prevalence of tricks

The sky of Banjul burns
And hot winds blow across the day
Infernal midday sun of dry season dances
Around the city, with catastrophic drought
At sight

There is pain and across just like the weather
But across the road, not that far
Village chickens occasional dart across our humanly presence
While colourful birds continued in their melodies
There are signs of life in the rainfall season ahead

You appeared, bathed in sweat and dust
You came and whispered tears into my ears
I held you n my hands and cried out
Please practice patience
For love can be a prevalence of tricks
We all huddled in the flickering shadow of t
So also is this life

29/09/19
Banjul

Your face sparkled

Jabbar, your face sparkled
With a childlike love
And it faded
Coming this season
Just like the Gambian weather
Very unpredictable

I have attempted to use the barometer,
You gave me to measure the season,
It reads stranger than fiction, your face
And as your river Gambia flows backwardly
With very rocky waves, never seen before

I can't doubt, unlike then
That our cuckoo clock is ending the story
Of our shared laughter and tears, at the foot of your bank
With this winter afternoon before us
It is stranger than fiction, your face

I don't need your barometer nor a weather prophet
To know that the sun has turned dark in the after
With this winter afternoon before us
It is stranger than fiction, your face

I woke up

I have shared laughter and pains with you
But
I walk alone along the flow, waves of
River Niger smiling at this prodigal

I woke up
I saw you from far
Lost in tears
Living in a separate world of yours,
And without mine

I listen to your fading talk, far from the mist
Hummmm
Is this reminiscing, or another night daydreaming
Of your fading self as a shadow at the dusk

But then
When the vital clues of our sun
Fade away with your smile at the bank
Of your smile coast,
Bank of the river Gambia

Oh soxna!
But indeed
Daydreams are tonic of good too
Bringing back strong image of you to me
As I watch the river Niger waves its waves across the tide
Oh my soxna, the strong evidence of my step at the smiling coast

Oh, more so, now the Niger weeps, it weeps for its prodigal
It calls me back to my toe

I woke up

Here I am
At the bank of my river Niger
Here I am
I see your antennae from far
And my senses are tuned to your wave, waiting
To see, hear and sense
Everything revolving around you, my run away love

10/09/19

Let us just kiss and say goodbye

I have felt your friendliness, and stuck to you
Now the winds of the Atlantic are blowing
In a dissimilar direction
I feel curious at this, as this river flows away from me
I feel less reassured standing at the bank of the river I had known
I feel less fine finding the known direction to your heart, once mine

Now it's feeling of
Lethargy, boredom, discouragement
Exhilaration, anxiety, above all and more
All written on once our sky ….
Can I still feel stuck to you
Watching your river flow, depressed and engulfed in self piety
Looking up, I recall the shared times,
We had holding each other as one
Imaging myself in you, you in me

But the time has come, time to let go
Playing background music with quick tempo
And outside, no birdsong, for the birds that had
Watched this love, had all gone, and at sleep; a sign
That I truly had to let go, shift gear, and face another direction
Before then, soxna, let us just kiss and say goodbye!

21/09/19

Moments of Doubts

Too strong to ignore

The placed promised us smiling coast
It is attraction too strong to ignore
Attracting whites and blacks
And like others, the songs of her birds were
Too strong, for me, to ignore
And the smiles coming from its tilapias too

Like the others, I jumped to its waters
And now am mourning my wounds!

19/08/19

Harmattan dusk

harmattan dusk came early
last year
mixing the day
with dusk and sneezing
there's a comma to the rain,
and each road
in my village
wears the plants with brown
puts period to their growth.
Now
signs are afar
to punctuate the dusks
with nature's bath
greeny
leafy
smile filled
exclamation mark!

18/8/19

As you slide away

I saw your gentle touch slide down my skin
Flowing away as it went by
Too quickly and smileless to hood
I saw you walk away, slide down into another skin
I saw the magma move
It pushes up
It pushes up on the plates
And the magma found a crack between the plates
Then spurt!
I had seen your fiery river too, had waited
Waited for the lava to cool
I called, and called
Your silence an answer to my calling
And my hoarse voice like that of a woman
Mourning her husband
I think I must go home
And forever to be gone
For my Niger beckons me home.

18/8/19

Our happiness

Oh my river Gambia, my woman, I have
Known your fear and hopes
Rise to the sun with a sonnet

I have seen such fears, rise
Across the flow of river Niger
Planting love down its bank, and
It sprouts; it grows!

I have seen such fear kiss hope
And a bright new sun blossoms

Oh my river Gambia, my woman, with this silky
Touch, though of a stolen moment, let me remove
Your fears, and for our longings

And we reap our dreams in this stolen moment!

19/08/19

Geej Gambia dafa nob geej Niger

The river Gambia was icy
This April morning

I tried to flag your sail off boat
As I arrived at that nearly forgotten visit

Waiting for our new summer to dawn
As without your smile

Everything was a cloud of mist

And you pulled the rope of an iron bell
And your boat full of smiles came out of the mist

My jabbar
River Gambia dafa nob river Niger*

20/08/19

1

---

*River Gambia loves river Niger (Wolof)

Stolen moment at the river Gambia

Am I human too
Actual being
In this dangerous embrace of snake and scorpion
Standing in this secret flow of this unfamiliar river
Somewhere yes back I dare not explore
But here I am alone in this dancing of river
Hiding my own secret at the bank of the river
As it flows away with my secret hiding sensations
But the scene and keeping coming back through invisible voices
Oh voices flow away as the river do

As my smiling coast turns up a jarring invisible voice

I know I have ventured into a perilous arm
My constant swear there as witness
But out of the blue, the recurring wind blew your smile across
It sang with the loudest song of dreaming of you
Terminating the perilous venture and the invisible voice
Am ever surrounded by your presence

Now that am back at the foot of river Niger
A thousand tons of thought at this moment of dream
In this solitary moment, yes a wild solitude and dreams
Fearful too, fearful revealing our shared secrets
Flowing with the flow of our river Gambia
I sat with this shaking uncertainty but dreaming of your river flow

I've been at the river bank sharing stolen moment

It has been most fearful to be

28/08/19

It's time to go back to river Gambia

Tonight is fearful, indeed
As I walk back alone to your bank
In dreams of you without you along river Gambia

Suddenly
I saw a star with swollen breasts,
Chased away by a moon in that darkly night
And it turned violent, bloody and red

Before I could know it
It's a humid morning
With your face appearing on my handkerchief
Nesting in the emptiness of my thought
I knew you were not where I left you behind

Then an owl of the marsh began to cry, it cried
The owl and its cry confirmed my fear
I then know it's time to go back your smiling coast
In search of that old matinee idol, I left behind
At the bank of the river Gambia

30/08/19

Days after Ramadan

The city is filled with familiar smiles again
As round the roads of Banjul all smiles with the sun
The natives and tourist laughed out the heart in the sun

Donkey heavy with loads
Struggle round the roads
Sweating round the roads

White uncontrolled beautiful cows
Flow and flow across the roads
Basking too in the sun along the roads

The city is filled again with smiles
As young damsels display their wares
Unwrapped for all to see along the roads.

05/09/19

Scar for the wrong reason

I have stood
At your door step
Too long a time but scared
For what I don't know, maybe
For the wrong reason

I drank from river Gambia
And hung my cup is a strange tree
With this strange affection, from
This stolen time, stolen moment, stolen dream

The betrothal belling is ringing
That is my precarious faith

05/09/19

Moment of doubt

You have borne fruit for me in dreamland
I cannot sleep again the whole night, nightmare
Of fear of you always present in my thought nightlong
Thinking of you flows naturally
As the water in river Gambia do
There you are, frowning, paying no attention,
And watching me suffer this all alone

The river Niger had through its water priestess
Had shown this earlier to me
I had the red and white signals flowing
From the deviations waving warning of waves
As I flow, deafly to the doorstep of your bank
I, a stranger at the coast of this smiling coast,
I'm really a stranger here
And you have led me into sinning against my land,
Its river and its great call

I have known, not today, even before and after, that
Love does strange things to strangers at a borrowed smiling coast
The lover turned turn, in wait of love
But love lean on faith to glow
Even at moments of doubt such as this.

12/09/19
Ikeji Arakeji

When I first saw you

Standing at the bank of river Niger
This early sun filled morning
The waves of river sing new songs of wave
Beautiful and refreshingly, but
There I am, but not there
As my emotion run fast to you
Just like a brakeless vehicle on a highway
This emotion, mine, with a movement
Of feelings, shared feelings, winged
Like that of colourful giant butterfly;
Winged, carrying my feelings
Just as in dreams across
The air, and the water, and to you

Why not
My whole heart is where you are
For you and I, love each other
Not minding we had drank from different rivers
This love is tendering stronger
When true love is honest, clothing no disguise
And left under the sun to shine, the more.

21/09/19

A Big Tear on My Face

Ungerminated seeds

what a wasted journey indeed
again and again
I have planted ungerminated seeds
At your river bank
As testament of our meeting
but Jabbar
your touch has gone sliding, sliding by
with this your new hiding in canyons dry
your touch slide into the night black sky
as I mourn the ungerminated seeds at your bank.

18/8/19

The flower I love gone

What a rain
Last night rain too heavy
To be imagined;
It shook everything at sight
My just like a hibiscus flower
In the sun fades away

22/09/19

Xenophobia

Can I call this an infection?
Or that you are a copy-cat
Since the ugly drums of xenophobia
The river Gambia flows not to my smile

Two of us had met
And danced to the lonely lovers' dance, sweetly without the sounds
You and I, all alone to our fantasy, borrowed and sweet

Then came the plague from Soweto, and its sibling cities
And you forgot our last dance of love
By the shores of your smiling coast

You have ignored our promised paradise, the mutual dream,
Sharing the pleasures of the lips together, in this borrowed moment
Lost in thought, lost in wonders, as love birds do

Soxna
What you do now is strange
It leads us to suffer further humiliation.

12/09/19
Ikeji Arakeji

A big drop of tear

You left on my pillow
That your big drop of tear
An indelible mark
Of your smile turned sour

I tried last night to erase it
And it turned red and blood
As it stared colourlessly at me
Leaving to more tears on my face

Let the Niger flow
And the Gambia too
And let us meet at where their dreams meet too
Sharing sunlights of birdsongs

Today's wind is dry, and cold, and sour
It turned violent without your leaving smile
At your river Gambia smileless at its coast
O' my jabbar: nama nala

Nwaanyi •
This land has seen many of our fights
It will see more too
But when your smile turns sour
on vacation must love proceed.

17/8/19
•

• Jabbar nama nala (Wolof – Gambia and Senegal): Wife I miss you.
Nwaanyi (Igbo – Nigeria): Woman

Just like an eclipsed sun

Cloudy yet
Woke up and watch
The perforated moment
As the river Gambia flew away
From my feet, staring with the candour
Of an extracted tooth

I thought I had planted taproot
At the feet of your river
And hooked you to my Niger
But look there
The river Gambia is black and drier
Without my tilapia
And I stand
A robot

I sing again of you, Jabbar
With unscanned balladry
As I watch the reeds of your Gambia
Today
Remembering that
She is warmless like an eclipsed sun.

18/8/19

Like the wind rattling

This morning a rattling wind knocked at my door
It roared and roared like a rude boy
Raging through the darkness of being without you
I wake up; knowing my chick is the talon of that hawk in flight!

18/8/19

And the coast is smiling less

I had taken it for granted,
But here I am, standing at the coasts with its rough beaches
And the coast is smiling less, and it's not smiling as dreamt

My dream of your touch varpourised
Like spirit left uncared for in the sun
And differed promised at the foot of dawn

I know that your river Gambia
And my Niger never will meet
To flow.

19/08/19

Sweet melodies out of the river Gambia

My jabbar
Your coyly, is river
Watering the bank of a tasty soul
But I make no secret of
My lifelong fear of water
As I stand before your presence
Oh my river Gambia

Lost, lost once again
I dreamt afternoon night dream
A sorrowful dream, of river Gambia loving river Niger
At the foot of your smiling coast
And your beauty came before my presence
And it touches me with the touch of laughter
And it wakes me up into another dream
As your beauty came before my presence
And shone and shone as a priceless stolen diamond
But it soothes my worried soul

And now waking up in another dream
I can hear your birds
And their throaty songs of sonnet and their sad melodies
I can feel you and feel your touch in this dream walk
Flowing out of waves of river Gambia.

20/08/19

I knew you were not where I left you

Distance and its close brother, time
Has continued to deny me your presence, as
I try to find you in shapes of your photographs

Watching many presences past with the flow of my Niger
And the winds of the waves flow with much beauty to behold
But suddenly there and behold a tattered roof in the star, of us

Trapped in a cancerous past, dying but stronger than grip of death
I stood up; wipe my eyes, walked away
I knew you were not where I had left you

30/08/19

For I have had enough today

I have been dreaming of you, soxna*
Have been washed away, because of you, just like seashells
On the riverbank, lifeless and colourless
Not only long but frosty feelings of our shared dreams
Butterflying in and around my skin

I have voyaged, and blindly too, but willingly
Between the shores of the rivers Gambia and Niger
You are in me, and I have you in my thoughts
With this endless dream butterflying inside my stomach
And my eyes become a dreamless gelatin

Soxna*,
I have come back to you, with this epic of dreams,
Luxuriating in your slippery arms
Without my regalia, a stranger on the smiling coast, songless
As thought of you has brought forth feelings in me
And words, the words of a poet imprisoned in huge silence
These words in my heart restless against cold marble
Are still erupting lucid and imaginative
Words of myths, of love and dreams; and of
River Gambia kissing my river Niger

I smile

I close my eyes, seeing
You as a blackbird perching on my window, beautiful
It's you, flowing with the waves

Oh my blackbird
There is no I
Without the you
For your image, beyond my touch, is just like a vapour

Cycling round and round in the wild wind

I wake up this midafternoon, and
The Niger calls again
With a stronger call this time around
I must leave, and I shall be lonely
Haunted by vapoured days of you
And the strong striking dreams of holding you

Fly away
Oh flow away and away river Gambia
For I have had enough today

She too is not alone

Rains are here again, it is rainy both smilingly and sadly
But our bush paths are evergreen, full of blooming hedges
The lonely owl perched at a tree trunk socked and sad
The butterfly flies round the nectar of nearby flower

She sat at the usual river bank, lonely, socked like the owl
Watching expectedly sad, hapless, counting her loveless lost
From the effect of the intoxicating nectar from her lover
As aching weariness engulfed her chubby face, smile starved

I watched too, as her strange feeling creep away from her face
With the quickness of the flower from the river Gambia into the Atlantic
Then I remembered that I too, like her, have seen this rain
And embraced the loveless breast of love in between

She is not just alone in the ever present lost battle of love.

02/09/19

Soxna, Let Me Go

Unbound me, let me go

Our days together, like half spent moon, cannot shine as before
It has gone too far to reverse, you and I now in the baboon-dog dance

As I look far beyond your face,
I see bold burden of unslept eyes
The phosphorescent beam of you, of love gone
but here I am, lost in the dance of forgotten steps
I dance to the wistful songs of the shadows of your eyes

I see clearly shadows of rainbows of love, spent dreams and tears
Seriating the furrow of your faces
Yes I see the rainbow of love above your shadow
But in no too distant a time, it disappeared

Here I am alone, wondering for love, your love

The river Niger, though far, still waits for the return of its prodigal
It is still calling and calling for the return of its own, its prodigal
I have hesitated for too long to harkens to this call
For I have been bound to you by love
My umbilical cord buried in your breast

Soxna, unbound me, set me free and let me go
It is time to embrace the call of my river Niger

26/10/19

You and I in this dream

What a day it is
With the sun's face in a hide and seek affair
Our day has refuse to brighten up, maybe
Because your absence is here present

Soxna
It has been a full moon now
And I have behold your face only in dreamland
With your now perpetual absence a continual decimal

It tortures just like the pangs of prison, I suffer
And loneliness betroths the wind
Thinking, and worrying my order of the day
I have once more vowed to behold your face

Soxna
Love is a sweet killing poison
If two lovers are together or not, not withstanding
It kills, more so loving from a distance

But you know
That your absence burns my heart
And the river Niger cannot tie me
Even with its luxuriating flow

Here I am, waiting for your smile, and my river mocks me
They laugh at me cause of quest of your smile in this midst of smiles
I suffer now this foolishness
Ehm a good play to live with as an art of love

If I tell you soxna
That is sad
Your leaving with sunshine of my heart

Behind the shadows of tears

But I know this
I know this is not an end
For the river Niger will surely meet the river Gambia
Then we embrace, and you out of that dream, and we are alive!

3/11/19
Lagos

Your silence will hatched to a song again

Song-bird wakes me this dawn
Looking out of the window, behold
The sun as pure as a cycle of gold
And the sky flowing live river of dawn
I woke up without my you there for me
There has been now song in this valley
Except that of your absence, it is a sour song
of the past with no voice to sing it
I am here dreaming of the future song
Of you in me sets in wings of the kites
And basking in promises that you made
At the bank of river Gambia
I wait looking out at the songless sky
Maybe beyond
In hope that your silence will hatched to a song again

3/11/19

Hopeless despair

The flow seems to draw me
To this pitiless breast
From an unsteady hand, your hand
Of a sentimental pretence

You, soxna
With this your display
Before the sun sets at dawn, of
Selfish disregard of love

I have seen enough
Of smiles clothed in secret soured love
In this our dance of disgusted tango
When love turns sour, turns loveless

I don't need further whispers
Unambiguous understanding of the colour of true smile
When love leaves, it leaves, and yours too far gone
Making its way back downriver

Neighbours my flower that is in my hand
Had faded its colour, brownish and dead
And the veil moved off my eyes

I stand in a hopeless despair!

3/11/19

Nature

nature

looking at nature's smiles
and its unimaginable beauty
at the red small fish swimming
round and round in the blue water
and the early sunshine mirrored in the water
red just like the small red fish
right at the tree behind, came the songs
beautiful songs of colourful birds
flowing out like from the hands of
perfectionist organist of old
sister see beauty in the sun, at display
weaved by divine creativeness
see beauty, such display of colours and sound
making life too elegant to preserve

I then looked into your eyes
I then saw colours of rainbows
I have seen them before, I saw them
when we had sat at the bank of your Gambian river
when you had said: I love you too

22/09/19

Early morning rain

It rained heavily this morning
With showers, strong winds and sandstorm
And the wind with big strong hands shaking everything
At sight. There I perched.
It rained, strongly
And a bird in its apartment is drenched
But it continues to sing sweet songs in that rain
Sweet birdly songs even in that heavy morning rain!

(*Banjul, 23/09/18*)

Author's Note

I feel that I should share this interesting discussion I've just had with a friend regarding the poem, Early Morning Rain. He wants to know why I ascribe 'apartment' to the bird nest and use the word: "perched" for my own lodging – when it should be the other way round. Interestingly the inversion of rhetoric, which literature professionals call hypallage or transferred epithets, is not uncommon in poetry. My case intends interposing our different positions so that while the bird is at much at home, I am miles away from home, in a hotel. So the bird is in the comfort of its home while I am in a borrowed home or, rather, a hired home. Incidentally we both had flown into our respective abodes before the rain – that heavy rain. Since the bird is very much at home it has less to think about, while, as a stranger in another land, I am in thoughts of home, wondering whether the heavy rainfall with all the winds is also lashing upon my beloved and ever flooded city of Lagos. I am also thinking family, hence while the bird is drenched in the rain, it has fewer worries still, so it could sing and sing. This is not the case with the traveler. His is the burden of travel. Travel, with thoughts of home, thoughts of family, hence he cannot sing!

Banjul this afternoon

I can't comprehend this weather
as the sun goes laughing
in this cold round the town,
the birds off the sky and songless, but
the roads are colour mixed – blacks and whites.
While blades of grass ice flattened down.

This is cold is killing
imprisoning me to my jacket, yet
the whites and natives seem to celebrate it; same
with fewer birds with green and yellow throats, &
for the hens uncertain of their notes.
This is weather reminds me of Naija* and its blessing.

5/5/19
Banjul

*Naija means Nigeria

Life

Light fades away
Like hibiscus flower
We fall back to sand

5/5/19
Banjul

Without a blanket

stepping out
in the street
this noon time

cold breeze
fights heats
of the non smiling sun
and the ground is cold

here am i
a witness
without a blanket
and in and outside
there are teardrops of cold

11/05/19
Serrankunda, The Gambia

Ramadan in Banjul

The street is cold as the season
everywhere is half empty,
like the marble head
the ladies covered up to the eyes
the bliss of music off, no more bliss
as all roads begin and leads to Ramadan

this can't be the Banjul, I know
lifeless, without usual colour, as
most drinkhouses dissolve,
then the beaches without water
as in dreams fraught
with irrevocable gestures,
yes the street is cold as the season
tis prayerful and peaceful too

5/5/19
Banjul

Work to do today

Just with a light rain
And early morning songs, sweet
Songs from the birds
Today begins as a day
After the cock crow at dawn

The sun came thereafter
And it smiles, and the sun smiles at the day
I heard a call of duty, of nature, and of work
The duty call to obey

For there's work to do today!

13/09/19
Ikeji Arakeji

Oh wind of kindness

The tiger stretched out on my way of survival
And I met a man who denied me gun to kill my tiger
Treading rough roads and having dreamt bad dreams as I move;
Both have given me sweet voices pushing on my dreams

But you gave me barometer and raingauge to measure my weather
You‘re my wind of kindness, blow on oh wind of kindness

01/06/18

Let it rain

As we wait for the rain
Shall we not receive it with sad smiles
From fears of great flooding
And damages of roofs
Shall we not mourn its aftermath
Not minding the presence of now parches across the land

Although we have waited this long
With prayer filled up lips for you
All through the days gone
Shall we receive the weeping of the earth
With great smiles
And arm full of blessings

Shall we not go back
And ask why these destructions and seeking damages
For the drumming on our rooftops
Or saying: sweet is that has come
Blessed is its sender, and blessed we are

Let it rain, again and again
Cool the earth

The heat has hanged heavily
Over our eyes for too long

30/08/19

Dawn of a dazzling sun

I have watched the rainbow
Disappeared by the appearance of the sun
Watched the Ramadan ram cried
Its last cry, and blood splashed from the cut of the knife
I have also heard the songs of the early morning birds
Welcome the dawning of the new day
Witnessed the rain cool mother earth surface

I have seen all these seasons, and smile

But the dusk is still around at dawn
And the songs of hope yet to come, after all
Days of trail, and promises denied
Then I have taken my big cross, heading on, I will go
As dawn, my dawn will give birth, a hope,
To a dazzling sun of tomorrow.

First draft 08/09/13 but rewritten 19/08/19

Prayerful

We forget too soon

Blessed is he
Who shares his smiles
Giving others smiles
As sunshine to live with

Bless me too lord
To have same sputtering flame of love
As I journey this earth with white hairs of age
To love others as self
Whether in return or not
So that my harmattan of years to come 'll be less cold

I have seen the stars come and go
All below the ground in wakeless sleep
And I have seen the few, leaving behind their love
Living beyond their own graves of sleep

Our quest for all of us is for us all alone
Evolving off from that lack feeding from our greed and envy
Oh
What an unbearable life to live
And an apt pity for not to admit

Lord
Pray I this day
Let me a giver
Of love and all worthy to give
Wherever I go
Let love flow from heart as
The river Gambia flows into the Atlantic

For I know this
The reward of love

Is tenfold that of not loving
Severally we have seen this
But easily forget same too soon

31/08/19

Sacrificial giving

Our dustbin
The receiver becomes
When we give
What we don't need

Giving
A sacrificial thing
It should be
With our sweat and blood
Flowing out of this.

29/09/19
St. Kizito's Catholic Church Serrankunda

Acts of love

There is neither beast nor beauty
All but beautiful hearts
To behold

All depends on
Who touches the heart

Meaning a smile
A token for the right mind

Our bound
Our note
Our knot

So hold on to love
For an endless love
To have

For a heart
As dear to me
As dear to all

12/10/19
Banjul

You are Lord Indeed

Beneath the shade, of lust and sins
Stream of memory recall, am dumbed, in sins
But your blazing love shone fo forgiveness
I shall come to thee with my dust, O' redeemer
For your love, strong, majestic and magnetic

I will leave this prison of mine, and run to thee
So shall I kiss your ever wounds, wounded for me
I will run to thee, lord, ever redeemer
In confession of sin with my rustic tongue
And acceptance of my wrong adventures
Before your presence, I join to proclaim
YOU ARE LORD INDEED

22/09/19

Obinna Chilekezi is a multi-skilled professional with background in library science, book publishing, finance and banking, marketing, and insurance. He was once the editor of _Nigeria Insurance Digest_ published by the Nigerian Insurers Association and had won the African Insurance Association award with one of his published books, _Marine Insurance: An Introductory Text_ in 2016. He is currently an insurance researcher and consultant, having worked in various arms of the industry. His poems have appeared in many journals and anthologies.

www.ingramcontent.com/pod-product-compliance
Ingram Content Group UK Ltd.
Pitfield, Milton Keynes, MK11 3LW, UK
UKHW042012190726
13854UKWH00005B/2261

9 789789 186037